MY ANGEL IS YOU

Nancy Barbee

Illustrated by
Kathryn Pope

Thank you
for being an
angle to the world.
Nancy Barbee

In loving memory of the many

angels that have gone before us.

This book is dedicated to two

such special angels;

Donnal Kennedy Harriett

Terry P. Titus.

Your whispers were miracles.

Gone too soon.

The child came with a question as children sometimes do. "What is an angel mother?" he asked. "And where and how and who?"

His mother took no heed to

what he really meant,

But gave a quick answer and

on with her work she went.

She told him, "Angels are in heaven

watching over us all.

They keep us in their sights and

protect us when our backs

are against the wall."

"So angels watch over us and

keep us from harm?

And they live in heaven?

Are their bodies warm?"

"I am busy now with washing your clothes

and making up the beds.

Go out and play with your friends.

Stop worrying

about angels."

she said.

So the boy took his favorite toy and went

outside to think.

As he looked in the sky a bright light

appeared, making him blink.

He looked away from the light and quickly hid his eyes.

A voice spoke softly, though sounded very wise.

"So you want to know about angels and where they come from? Lets look all around you and see if we can find one."

"Yes, there are angels in heaven

that watch over you as you sleep.

They look like the pictures you have seen

in books, and when you are hurt, they weep.

But did you know

that angels live right here on earth,

and help you along your way in finding

your own self-worth?"

"What do you mean?" the boy asked.

"And how can this be so?

Angels have wings and wear white gowns

and their heads have a halo.

How can there be angels here on earth?

I have not seen them here.

Do they hide when I'm around?

Do they live in fear?"

"Oh no. They do not hide, but they

are with you wherever you go.

Maybe it is because you do not see them as

angels, but would like to know?"

"Oh yes please tell me where I can find

them?" the boy cried with glee.

"So I will know who they are and keep them

close to me."

The voice spoke softer and said,

"Let me ask the questions now."

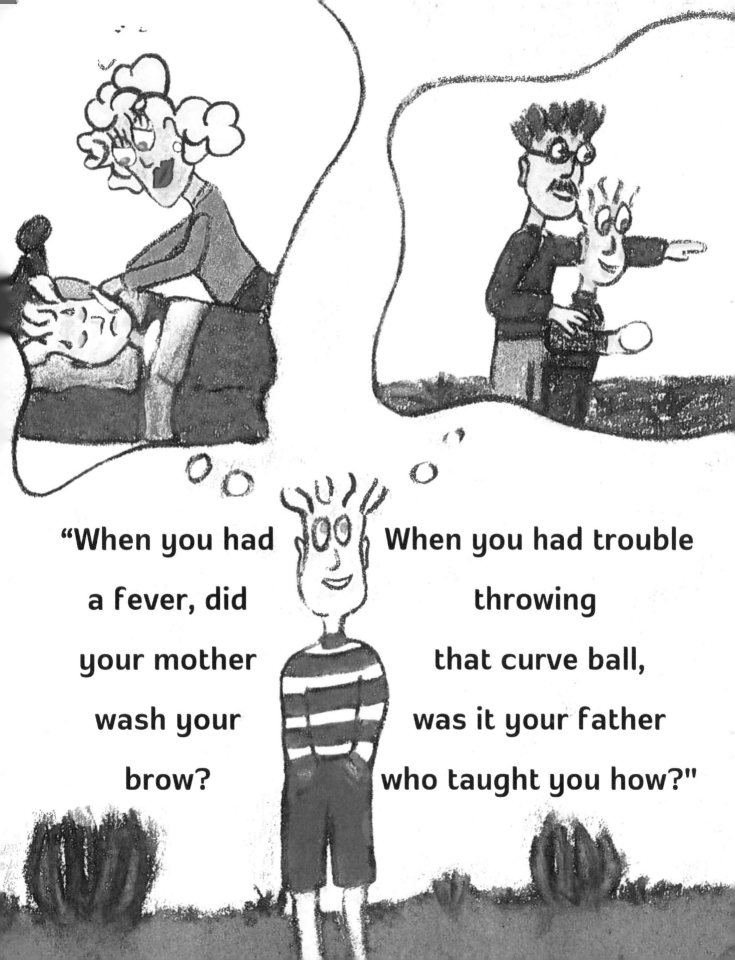

"Did your teacher in school

make you behave and teach

you how to read?

Did your grandmother give you a love of

plants and show you all about seeds?"

"When you burned your hands on those very

hot coals, who ran to get your mom?

Who stayed by your side at the doctors and

tried to keep you calm?"

"That was my best friend." he said.

"But, how did you know?"

"Wait! A few more questions

before I have to go.

When a stranger has shown you kindness

or given you encouragement,

isn't the stranger a gift from God straight

from heaven sent?"

"Did you ever

feel so alone

and wonder

what was wrong?

Was it your

grandpa who

came to keep

you company

and pushed

you along?"

"Oh yes." said the boy,

"All of this is true.

Angels do live in heaven.

My special angel is you."

"Angels live right here on earth

and teach me everyday

how to become a man and

help me along my way."

"Yes." said the voice.

"You finally understand.

If I were right beside you,

I would shake your hand."

"Listen to those who come into your life.

They are there to teach.

For they are your angels here on earth,

and they will help you reach

your highest goals or wildest dreams all

that you can be.

By knowing them, you finally will know me.

Tell me about your angels.
Share your story with me here:
nancybarbeebooks@gmail.com

CPSIA information can be obtained
at www.ICGtesting.com
Printed in the USA
BVHW011030160323
660593BV00008B/600